WINGS OF FREEDOM

PAPIA RAY

INDIA • SINGAPORE • MALAYSIA

ISBN 979-8-89446-982-9

Introduction

Writing poetry has always been my pleasure. Wings of Freedom is a compilation of my poems written over the years. Nature is a constant presence as also human nature. It's true that as one writes one learns. So keeping to the rules of rhyme and rhythm and also breaking them has been an enjoyable journey for me. Free verse is my comfort area, my wings of freedom. Some poems may require loud reading to be enjoyed in full. Part 1 consists of the types of verses, which expand, in full varied forms in Part 2. May the reader enjoy reading both.

The Author.

Contents

Verses in different forms   23

Part 1
Types of Verse

1. Monostich

i.   Be my sunshine in my sunless world.

ii.   I saw a family picture among the heap of bricks
and mortar.

2. Couplet

i.   How through life and living we try to seek that
haven called childhood

And yearn awhile to bask in the shade where
tranquility once stood.

Many a time we look here and there and wonder
what we miss so

They are those half-forgotten links severed long
ago.

ii.   Through the shattered window she saw

A soldier limping, his wounds raw.

Thick smoke and total destruction

He seemed a ghost in her garden.

His gun was slung from his shoulder

And his cap pulled over an ear.

He was alone, his mate was gone

Half buried in her garden lawn.

The badges on his chest shone bright

As they gleamed in the hazy light.

The blood oozed out on to the ground

As a wall crumbled without sound.

The soldier now had reached her door

It had fallen the night before.

She stood still by her shattered window

A brave little soul in the shadow.

3. Tercet

i.   Good health and happiness can come your way

If you can follow some rules everyday;

Get up at dawn, smile at all, at night pray.

A brisk walk, appreciating nature

Sensible diet, greeting your neighbour,

Can only add to your life, much flavour.

ii.   Remember me not when I am all dead

Remember me now when I'm here instead.

There's much to talk, so much what's left unsaid.

I have waited and shall wait forever,

'fore the new moon rises and thereafter,

I'll be there as always. Just remember.

The moon has risen above the palm tree

A silver arc beaming in misty sea

I wait, for that hour when you'll be with me.

I think I hear your footsteps approaching

Past and Present merge, Future's beckoning

Time stands still and the world's aglow, watching.

4. Quatrain

i.   High summer days

April, May and June

When the sun's rays

Start the day too soon.

Hot summer breeze

Early morning walks

Branches of trees

Form shadows on rocks.

ii. Of beauteous morns, wine coloured days

  Long languorous noons, spiced mango shakes,

  Star-filled evenings, iced lemon drinks,

  Still brooding nights, glowing firefly wings.

  Long before dawn the little birds sing

  The air is pure, the temple bells ring

  Languid rivers echo children's laughter

  The banyan tree spreads its shade all over.

5. Quintain

i. Don't be angry mate the traffic light is still red

  You are driving, so am I, both a fraction late.

  I cannot make way, don't you see? Would you jump the light instead?

  Don't honk, let's wait. Soon you'll take a turn and I shall race ahead.

  The traffic light you see is now blinking red!

ii.   Behold

        The monument

        That stands beside the sea

        Whose ancient walls still whisper of past

                Glory.

6. Sestet

i.   I heard the knock on the front door

        Who could it be at this unearthly hour?

        I wondered, waited, and heard repeated

        Three little taps, --- a pause. One more!

        Until I opened the door to see,

        A swaying branch gently nudging the door.

ii.   A vision she was in the first light of dawn

        Her face, unlined yet by day's toils,

        Her eyes, deep pools of innocence,

        Her smile, a rainbow of happiness,

        Her humming voice like distant temple bells

        Echoed a song long after she was gone.

7. Septet

i.   I sit in solitude

On a beach bereft of seagulls

A picture frame of quietude

With waves breaking my train of thoughts.

Like spirited horses they come

Exuding much froth and foam

To scatter around me as they come and go.

ii.   Have you sometimes felt a sense of awe while walking down

An old road of an old city?

Walked backwards in time down one of those infinite serpentine lanes

That knows no end?

Have you paused before grand, crumbling gateways that still hold

Bold marble engraved names?

Did you hear then, amidst the chaos and din, choked whisperings of stories untold?

8. Octet

i.   Sweet September, you stand in silence

      Wondering what season you belong to.

      Neither high summer nor breezy autumn

      You exult in the cool passing showers of departing monsoon.

      The sun shifts slyly to slant through the window

      Bringing the first feel of festive air and illumined skies,

      The rolling clouds, the lazy sun, the evening dew---

      Yes September, you mark the quiet passage of time.

ii.   There is a whole wide world waiting outside

      Open your window, look up at the sky

      In silence breathe, watch the eagle in flight

      And you'll find again your song deep inside.

      Set your thoughts free let your eyes wander wide

      When the trees sway, listen to what they say

      When the sun bows out, count the shades of light,

      In the growing gloom, there's a world outside.

9. Nonet

i.   Sit by my side and sing me the song

The one that we sang together

When days were lazy, nights were full,

And the moon was up at dawn.

Before the light of day goes out

Yet another time

Sing that song

Again.

Now.

ii. He was there reading a newspaper

And by his side stood a table

On the table was his cup

His cup of morning tea.

Its aroma spread

Magic unfurled

He read on

Sipping

Tea.

10. Decastich

i.   Let's walk through the woods on a bright summer day

And sit beside the stony brook

And watch the birds bathe and play

And splash about in a shady nook.

Let's walk on the loose, red earth that leads nowhere

And drink in the mellow sun

And feel the wind blow all day

See the squirrels turn and run.

Let's walk, and walk through the woods on paths unknown

Forever together, hand in hand.

ii.   City light

Blinking bright

Buildings old

Stand up bold

Bumpy roads

Honking cars

Roadside shops

Selling chops

In the light

Blinking bright.

11. Free verse

i. Behold, the beauteous moon

That shines yonder!

Bask in its sublimity

And let its magic potion

Seep into your soul;

Let tired hearts and hurt minds heal

And be forever free of earthly malady.

Behold, up there she shines,

An orb of silver and gold,

Raining rays of light and enlightenment

As she surveys her kingdom of night;

In silence she remains through the daylight hours

In silence she fades like a queen exiled,

Only to return in glorious splendour.

Behold, there she is, the beauteous moon!

ii. I have much time to spare,

To play the game of Add - Delete.

I click open that page of friends

To see them smile and celebrate.

As I scroll, you ask -How many? Two hundred, I say triumphantly

Fifty more to reach your number, let me see if there are any ---

Take your time, you say, as I stop momentarily

To take in the message that stares at me, a friend is no more friends with me!

Part 2

Verses in different forms

1. A Wish

Let

this world

fill with song

that will echo

and bring together

one voice to rise 'bove all,

one beat that will be heard long

and remembered through the ages

and voiced with awe and reverence.

With hands folded let us pray awhile

for that lost voice of sanity

to lead us and guide us back

to truth, righteousness,

to bloom forever

in the hearts of

millions

and more

souls.

2. The Letter

A letter lay on the table
Carefully placed under a book
The address was part visible
Yet no one even gave a look.

Carefully placed under a book
No hurried steps or excitement
No one even gave it a look
Or read the name for whom 'twas meant.

No hurried steps or excitement
No questioning glance turned that way,
None to read for whom it was meant,
It lay unclaimed throughout the day.

No questioning glance turned that way
It lay there supine and humble;
Unread, unclaimed throughout the day
The letter lay on the table.

3. The Sea

I stopped by for a while to soothe my soul

And watch in awe a calm, passionless sea,

Soon dusk descended from clouds black as coal

I stopped by for a while to soothe my soul.

As waves that gently peaked and fell did roll,

And sprawl with joyful ease in front of me

I stopped by for a while to soothe my soul

And watch in awe a calm, passionless sea.

4. Spring

I am Spring, receive me with open arms
Give me space, let me bloom and dance awhile,
Where are the trees and the beautiful farms?

The noise and the smoky air give me qualms
Barren fields stare, where the children, their smile?
I am Spring, receive me with open arms.

This sweet earth has been robbed of all her charms
Birds are gone, forests still burn by the mile.
Where are the trees and the beautiful farms?

I offer to you all my magic balms
All my colours, fruits and fragrance I pile
I am Spring, receive me with open arms.

Nature provides, yet men are up in arms;
Peace resides in every innocent smile.
I am Spring, receive me with open arms.
Where are the trees and the beautiful farms?

5. The Visitor

Softly lit by the setting sun, the room was neat and cosy

The visitor stepped in unsure, the host welcomed him warmly

Soft footsteps brought in the hostess, who approached quietly,

The host proudly introduced, 'Meet my dear wife, Geetanjali.'

The name warmed his being, the visitor got up hastily,

A pang of hope jabbed his heart as he looked towards the lady

And saw, the same proud head, the demure smile, the stubborn dark eyes

That once had spoken in silence long, but now looked at him gravely.

6. The Boats

The boats are waiting by the shore

The river calm in evening light

The ducks have all waddled ashore

The boats are waiting by the shore.

The mist now hangs upon the shore

The rising moon now fades from sight

The boats are waiting by the shore

The river calm in evening light.

7. O Boatman.

Find some time to sit by my side
I have many stories to tell
Since ages I have travelled far
Since ages I have carried your woes.

Long miles through valleys deep and far
Along lone village big and small
Through choking cities I have traversed
Listening to your same old song.

Through rocks and jungles I have meandered
Crashing down from mountains high
Through desert land I have wandered
Seen your struggles since ages long.

Sit by my side and share your thoughts
O boatman come, I'll bear you along
Row your boat on my swirling waters
And let's together sing your song.

8. My River

In and out, in and out, I paddle my little boat

Through inlets, outlets, round little islands

The boat is my home, my very own.

In and out, in and out, through thick, green paddy fields

I row my boat, my little boat, from early morn to sundown.

I stop to rest by the shore and sing my song to the benign moon,

Tales of horror, war and warrior, the boatman and his river.

Row, row, I row my boat cutting through storms and murky shallows

The boundless river is my wealth, I dwell in its shadows.

Row, row, I row my boat, bouncing along the rushing waters

I free myself and away I go, my river knows no borders.

9. The Eyes

Sitting several rows away, he saw her.

She sat alone, quite alone, perhaps a family guest.

Irresistibly drawn, he walked closer.

She turned. He stopped. No talk, no smile. Seconds passed.

He looked away, stung; seared, singed all through.

Such pain, such grief, such profound anger smoldered

In eyes so deep ----.

He walked away. No talk, no smile. Just guilt.

Why? Why? He wondered.

10. My Childhood Home

I had forsaken it for a career abroad

Lured by a jet-set life;

New horizons, new people

Money, temptations, never-thought-of indulgences

----.

Until one dusky evening

Came a bolt from the blue ----

A call from the past,

That struck with all ruthlessness,

Raking up settled memories, sentiments,

Long-forgotten values,

Guilt.

Across lands and oceans on another land

I found myself one dusky evening ------

Feeling my way through once- familiar paths ---.

Among the mad twitter in the trees and the blinking lights,

My unsure eyes searched in vain for familiar sights,

My eager eyes strained to hear sounds heard long ago ----.

Where was it?

I reprimanded myself.

Had I forgotten my way to my childhood home?

Where I had grown up -----

Running around, climbing trees

Flying kites, chasing bees?

The haunted neem of boyhood fancies,

The pond full of stars, the twin tamarind trees?

Where the green terrace door which could be seen from afar?

Instead, I stood dwarfed by a tall

Architectural splendour,

River View Tower.

11. My Goddess

The Goddess is here.

Yet, I seek my goddess.

I seek her in the misty slopes of silence

I seek her in the raging fire of violence.

I seek her in the lofty walls of religion.

I seek her in the whispered prayers of children.

Is she the spirit that soars in the sky?

Is she the laughter that dances in the eye?

Is she the shining blade of a sword held high?

Is she the parched lips of a soul about to die?

Is she the one I meet every day?

The one with matted hair and unquestioning eyes?

Whose battlefield is the pavement and her enemies strewn far and wide?

And her shield, her own undaunted spirit?

She, she is my goddess, I bow to her.

Battle-worn and fearless

She fights endless battles

Head held high, eyes ablaze,

Almost on her knee, but not quite ---

She, she is my goddess; I bow to her.

12. The Woman

A wonder of wonders is the woman.

Great Nature's gift to mankind,

A blessing to the world she lives in,

A permanent presence in every breath of life.

She has been here since time immemorial

Carving out success stories,

Reaching for the stars and claiming glory,

Fighting battles and making history.

She makes her voice heard on her hearth and outside

Against all deeds of every hue.

She succumbs to unholy whims

That rips apart her soul in two.

She burns; she drinks her pride and writhes in pain

Her ego nose -diving a thousand million times.

Silent tears burn her spirit to ashes

Churning and choking them into barbaric hues ---.

But then she rises and upward she soars

Into the vast expanse of the blue sky

Like the phoenix, indestructible

In her very garb of victory.

13. Sunset in the desert

The sky was afire

With sudden passion

As the sun bent down

To kiss the horizon;

Shades of orange

Pink and purple

Crossed each other in tumultuous fashion.

I sat among the golden dunes

Watching dumbly the play of hues

As Heaven's palette spilled over

Over the golden sandy dunes.

Sometimes a golden crest it was

Sometimes a heap of molten gold

And sometimes a silvery sparkling streak

That flashed like lightning from end to end.

I sat still in the desert stillness

As dusk spread a mysterious glow

The sun retired in quiet haste

In a blaze of glory like never before.

14. Death

Death, are you an imposter

Camouflaging your presence

Under a pseudonym?

Wielding your deadly baton

With mindless abandon?

Are you a mindless phenomenon?

Striking at will, at random?

When and as you please -

Your sole aim to make life cease.

You gatecrash with remarkable ease

Causing a ripple in the reigning peace.

Are you jealous of Life?

So eager are you to stop its sweet flow,

To cut short its eager steps,

To destroy the dreams just beginning to grow,

To pluck out the steady breath,

Of one, in the very pink of health?

Are you an answer to a prayer ---

Entreating you to play fair and square

And release life writhing in agony

Incarcerated in senility

Entrapped in inexplicable malady?

Are you a sadist?

Gloating at the mess of human stress

Smirking at the tears of helplessness

Until, Time takes charge

And begins unobtrusively her healing therapy

Soothing the heart, soul and mind

Into believing, that life is a dream -.

And you Death, a stark reality?

Or, are you a messenger

With promises of a life hereafter?

Ah, yes, you are the phantom

Seated on your high winged stallion

Holding the reins of Life

Descending from nowhere

Ready to strike

An unsuspecting soul.

Remove your veil

And reveal your true self

Be proud and proudly claim what is yours.

Do not sneak, for I am proud too

And know when to part

With that which abides in me

And which now I know no longer belongs to me.

I have a glimpse, a vista

Of a world that is soon to be mine

Of miles of heavenly-hued skies,

Of feather topped waves and sweet scented shine,

As I stand on tiptoe on the edge of the universe

In a state of ecstasy ready for flight.

Come, hurry, lift me up

Like a sip from the cup,

Like a leaf from the earth

And release me

Into the fathomless depths of Eternity.

15. Rohtang Revisited

I was there again one night

To look for a dream I'd left behind

In Rohtang, desolate and lonely with barely a
sound,

Except, for a soft gush the river made

Which mingled with the wind that whistled away

To mingle again with much flair

With my breath,

When deeply I breathed the frosty air.

I stood on the white slopes of Rohtang

Alone with myself on top of the world

In the middle of a desert

Made of marble and ivory

Under a calm and stormless sea,

Where the moon in a brilliant star-spangled sky

In ethereal grace was riding high

A luminous, familiar, ever-dear presence

With not a cloud to mar her countenance,

Where the massive mountains in the distance

Looked like hooded monks in deep meditation,

Their impassive forms as if etched in ebony

Against the glowing night-sky of Rohtang.

And softly I tread on the slippery ice

That glistened like glass in the mellow moonlight

Among the undulating slopes

When the first snowflake kissed my nose.

They fell like feather, like wisps of cotton

On me and around straight down from Heaven

Colouring my world with alabaster cream

Draping the moon, the monks, in mist and mystery.

With the monotonous monologue of the river

And the crazy wind whistling in my ear

In the woolly white I stood deep in the snow

Holding my breath still waiting for more.

And then all of a sudden

On the eastern horizon

The first flush of dawn

Announced another morn

And greeted me

On the snow-laden slopes of Rohtang.

The sky was blue, the moon was gone,

The hooded white monks looked solemnly on

As chilled to the bone, my mind in a whirl

I left that place with a song in my soul.

16. The Sword of Righteousness

Behold! Uphold my sword of righteousness!
Upright it stands, sword of valour, lightning bright
Remover of despair, true giver of joys.

I heard the words and beheld the wondrous sight
The voice too clear to be a distant dream,
The moon-flamed sky real with a moon so white.

The mighty sword stood on a floating moonbeam,
Unseen hands held it aloft, a burning torch---,
Mixed wonder gripped me as in a frightened dream.

And then I saw the mist rising from the gorge,
A vision of ephemeral translucence
With silver wings, flaming eyes, ready to surge.

My gun, a symbol of a killer's essence,
My army, like thundering waves, my power,
I aimed, ignoring childhood reading lessons.

Be still, Foolish Man, come down your high tower,

Hold still your restless feet, greedy hands, lewd
tongue ----

For they have razed this earth and shamed your
brother.

Your time is up and your final bells have rung ----,

The skies seemed to reverberate with fury ---

Mesmerized, I stood as to my pride I clung.

Accursed! Banished! Monstrous Death for
company!

Alas, for a balm to relieve my distress

A word, a flame, to guide me back to Beauty.

And in the light of dawn, I heard the voice bless ---

Behold! Carry this sword of righteousness!

17. Morning Brew

Shall I receive you with a rosy wreath?

Your sweet presence makes my mornings brighter.

The sun shines upon every home and hearth

Enriched by your aromatic flavour.

Unruly rains or sweeping gales cannot mar

The magic you wield on every mortal.

When caught by your lingering charm I swear

I forget my hour, place and my trouble.

You are my revered Darjeeling First Flush

My pot of brew in pretty porcelain,

When you sit in command there is a hush----

You cast a spell, and like a queen you reign.

Till the time dear earth bears you, gives you life,

Till then may you thrive and add life to life.

18. Tread Softly

Tread softly!

Here lies Death.

Nature weeps.

In the gathering gloom

Silent shadows mourn

The death of mighty Death.

No more a prayer on the lips of the tormented,

No more a bitter sweet potion from earthly pain,

No more a divine messenger cloaked in mystery,

Or the wise judge of grievous Life

Or the cool touch on the senile brow ----.

Now reduced to a horror game of will and whim

Death strikes with crazy ease.

Tread softly!

The once robust Life rests here.

The dying sun lingers.

Betrayed. Shocked.

Nature weeps.

Tread softly.

19. Shyam, the Fisherman

The banyan tree spreads all around
Its branches hanging down
Come let us sit and breathe its air
Before you go to town.

The children sat with eager eyes
To hear a tale or two
They liked the woman's long, grey hair
And loved her stories too.

Shyam the singer, shy and simple
He had a boat you know
That leaped through the choppy waters
Faster than an arrow.

His hut stood in his paddy field
His heart was in his song
Sweet jasmine he took for Matla
While fishing all day long.

One day he caught a haul of fish
And didn't know what to do
He shared it with the villagers
Cooked some for himself too.

And then one night a raging storm
The Matla in his hut
His little village seemed to sink
What curse was this, he thought.

His little boat lay just nearby
Shyam took some flowers in hand
Sweet jasmine to calm the river
That had encroached his land.

Shyam was a brave fisherman, yes
And a dare devil too,
He knew how to soothe the river
And try to tame it too.

As he faded into the night
Amidst loud cries of fear

He shouted back to all and near
I will be back, stay clear.

He walked in mud right to the edge
And bravely he did stay
The roaring Matla came to him
And dug him deep in clay.

Calm down, I offer sweet jasmine
Shyam said raising his hand
Take my young life if you want to
But do not take my land.

The Matla raised her head in awe
And saw his misery
The jasmine bright in gooey clay
The man in agony.

I have to tell his story though
I did promise him that
A thousand times this month of rain,
Or Matla will be mad.

The children looked at each other
Oh, what did Matla mean?
The woman stroked her long grey hair
That smelt of sweet jasmine.

Now you can go, I'll tell you more
Shyam loved his paddy field,
Tomorrow again, do come here
With garlands of jasmine!

20. Solitude

And there I was, alone with the sky

Alone with myself, on an upward climb.

I stopped to look at the day so bright

It seemed to breathe much joy and mirth.

The sound of a bee filled the balmy air,

The restful earth felt a cradle to me,

The breeze in gentle waves did move

Through trees along the undulating slopes.

Sunbeams sparkled in the distant grove

Where children's voice rose in lusty chorus.

I stood stunned as under a spell

Savouring this moment of solitude.

21. Sanctity of Marriage

By the holy fire they took their rounds,

Hearts in sync, as the priest the 'shlokes' chanted,

The sky gazed down at the ritual profound

The earth in grave silence watched enchanted,

The holy river calmed down and waited

Vedic chants, conch shells, incense filled the air,

As two minds merged, their lives to honour, share.

The auspicious hour, and Heaven beholds

The bride bedecked in gold and gorgeous red

The humble groom, solemn in silken robes,

Seven rounds, seven vows and then be wed,

Each a promise so remembered and said ----

Blessed by parents, wise words by elders too,

Friends to guide and cheer, they start life anew.

May their union bear fruit and bring joy

May their lives be full of laughter and cheer

May they enjoy each myriad moment

And face all adversity without fear,

May one hold the light so in dark see clear,

Through thick and thin and troubles that may come

May they, hand in hand bravely overcome.

22. Awake, dear Poet

Awake, dear Poet, awake from your eternal sleep.

Awake and lift your pen and wield it at your whim,

Bring back some guiding light to the world that's now so dim,

And with ardent Poetry save it from mires deep.

O, for a chance to read your thoughts more, and to query

The harsh syllables that portrayed your traumatic times,

Poetry you denounced, exalted prosaic lines

To etch War, Bloodshed and Famine's brutality.

O great Poet, in your countrymen's heart you abide,

Your works oft-quoted, but not celebrated alas,

Return, return to your land where your heart was,

Now free from shackles and holding her head with pride.

O cruel Death, to wipe out a life that was to start!

O cruel Life, to cease, to ebb away too fast,

Forsaking Youth that should have eighty summers last

And been blest by you, not like in jest torn apart!

23. The Masterpiece

(' The Glow of Hope' - painting by SL Haldankar)

Come this side please, miss not this masterpiece,

The Glow of Hope or, The Lady with the lamp,

Painted in nineteen forty five- forty six

It adorns this wall, haunts my mind's peace.

Do you see the shadow behind the girl?

So large, three times her graceful size I think,

And the light, that lights up the dark beyond

Also lights up her face, sweet Geeta's face.

Grave and sombre, daughter of the painter

She holds a tall, brass lamp lit up and bright.

Look, look! Her eyes----alive with many dreams

And her lips waiting for conversation.

Her saree, a delicate lavender

With a shade of pink and a gold border

Embraces her like a doting mother.

That little flame shining through her fingers---

For whom has she lit? For the temple gods?

Or, to welcome guests at her entrance door?

Perhaps, it is the night of Diwali?

The longer you stay the more she will tell

If you listen to the silence that's within.

Three hours at a stretch she has stood thus

For the painter to produce his magic ---!

Look--- that noble head on a slender neck,

The face all aglow with sweet innocence ---

Is firm as the lamp and the flame she shields.

Feel blessed in the presence of the painting,

Each stroke of the brush you must wonder at,

Bow to that moment of inspiration

That gave rise to this awesome work of art!

24. Choice

Verse through voice

Or voice through verse?

I can't decide

Help me please.

Faced with a choice

I weigh options.

Perhaps this

Or maybe that ----

That's life

I know that!

I become nervous

And toss a coin

Heads or tails?

Yes or no? ---

Again a choice

For me to choose.

Logic steps in

Voice through verse

That's it

Yes it is.

Rhyme or rhythm?

Both surely

Rhythm more ----

Or rhyme equally

Whatever ---

Words make verse

Words make this world

Do they? Not thoughts?

Come Logic!

Logic again?

Verse is not Logic

Neither is Life ---

Ok I accept

And rest my case

With much relief.

A niggling doubt ----

I squash it!

Voice finds its verse

And that's it!

25. My Desk

The magic that my glance each morning brings

Behold, there are so many little things

Shining in the morning light

Upon the desk painted white,

A glass paperweight, cube shaped, edges sharp,

Pins in a holder beginning to warp,

A diary full of scribble, a stray line on the cover,

Another below waiting, its pages seeking favour;

A dictionary sits spreading its weight

Beside a lantern like lamp standing straight,

A pen holder full of jotters, a bottle of water,

To keep all free of dust, a folded felt duster.

And now the reigning queen that occupies centre stage

Has been my companion since many, many days

And the little mouse that plays at her feet

Is the most active performing its feat.

The keyboard yes, is just below the belly

Lies in state when I'm watching the telly.

And on my desk you will find these things,

This list of things to connect my links;

Each one and all mean much to me

Much time I spend in their company.

26. Curse

Curse me not, O Life, I fail,

I fail to be the supreme self

That you wished for me when I first breathed

When you blessed me with all the best you have.

27. Morning

Come Morning, come and rest a while

Behind the clouds take shelter now

Let my true love think it's still night

Let blissful dreams be slow to bow.

As I leave, be slow to enter

Be slow to peep through the window

Let your touch be soft and tender

So when she wakes won't miss me so.

Dear Morning, I know it's your time

And time for me to leave her side

Duty calls and soon I must go

The clock denies the time to bide.

Come morning, come, light up the dawn

Gently spread your wings with the sun

Bid me a whispering farewell

'Cause I shall come when duty's done.

28. Dark Night

Dense, dark Night, lead me on

Through darkness, towards dawn

Through hazy mist, to the horizon

Through the mystery, to reason.

29. The House

I saw that house again; it is so dear to me

The road was busy and my legs they carried me ---

Amidst crowded concrete there she was like a dejected queen

The iron gate rusted, my head between the bars uproar within

The windows slatted green

My grandmom calming an agitated me

This garden this corner there used to be a mango tree,

Rain storms, mangoes falling, the door banged shut ---- empty

Empty. How so empty, but I see, I can see

Still see and feel those laughing times

Filling me ----

The faces round the table the tablecloth stained,

The hot food and a thin veil of smoke,

How it rained,

My mom's gold-bangled hand serves rice,

Uncle's crumpled nose, father grave

The mountains behind them --- I nudge my brother

Brave he was, so brave.

That window, that window on the right,

Yes, yes she smiles

The grey blue sky there's sunshine

In the jars of pickles

She waves her hand, her arm

In sleeves of lace so white

The red border frames her face, the diamond dot bright.

I am back from school,

A swing on the gate, parrots

The door opens, soft muddy grass, nibbled mangoes

She stands, the window bangs shut and the pigeons hover

The house so quiet now from what I remember.

30. Will you come?

will you come calling
when the wind chime sways gently
and the wind whispers

the time of day,

when dewdrops glisten
like diamonds in the sunshine
the wild blue jay calls

again

when in the autumn
the blue lotus blooms once more
in the empty pond

will you come calling?

31. The Bridge

One rainy day on the bridge, watching the river flow,

I chanced to hear your name repeated like an echo;

Alone I stood, till stars were out and began to glow,

Upon a silent shadow, where once we'd stood before.

Remember how we matched our steps, with every ripple,

The river flowed sedately, singing a careless trill

We walked so hand in hand, in summer time and winter,

The cuckoo cooed, we twirled, as did the gurgling river.

Our hearts were young, with hands entwined, we dreamt aplenty,

The promises were not enough, they were so many;

They withered in silence dear, in silence we shall cry,

In silence we shall part, in silence wave a goodbye.

And still I wait a shadow still, perhaps for a chance,

To hold your hands again in mine, for that promised dance.

32. Where are they?

Where, where are they, the children?

Is it not their time to play?

The evening breeze blows cool

The sun daubs the horizon---

Where, where are they? Where?

The robust boys, their proud football?

What day is today? Sunday?

Wednesday, did you say?

Still the parks so empty, so empty, why?

The swings, slides, that guava tree,

The green grass patch --- so barren, free?

No laughter, no running feet

No cries of pain, triumph, defeat?

Yes, --- those little girls, their dolls,

Who played hide and seek, hopscotch,

Fond of coffee sets, lipstick ---

Are they too lost in those games

That start, end, with a click?

33. Regal Teak

Who shall sit around me today? I wonder.

Suited and booted and oiled and well powdered ----

Will they be friends and foes? Or friends' friends?

Or foes' foes?

But still together?

Presidents or Prime ministers?

Chairmen then? Or, Comrades?

Shall I hear their polite gabble in anger?

How many will come? How many shall lean on me?

With papers and files and needless jabber

To talk and repeat, to talk and repeat

With no hint of any solution ever

Oh my! You cups and cups and pots and pots of pretty porcelain,

What do you do on my top of polished lavender?

What foolish talks do you hear all day from lips that sip?

From lips that sip and slip and flip and break into feigned laughter?

See? Neat hands that shake and shake for the cameras?

A million clicks! Do they click you? No? Not me either.

Where were you before? I was a regal teak growing wild,

And where I once stood now stands a high barbed wire.

It stretches for miles and miles and grows high with every talk,

But not as high as I used to be. I was still higher.

34. O Night

O night, in your soft embrace let me lie,

Cry,

With sad thoughts I seek comfort and ease,

Peace.

Away from day's chaos let me stay

Pray,

And awake with moonlight on my face.

Trace

In intricate patterns my fond dreams,

Teams

Of shadows let flit in valleys deep,

Heap

On me your magic charm forever,

Ever,

O night, in your soft embrace let me lie,

Sigh.

35. Footsteps

Whose footsteps still echo here like before?

For

years ago, one bright summer noon you,

You

went out that door and never returned,

Turned

the clock upside down and time stood still,

Still

as the Buddha on the mantelpiece.

Peace

returned to my life and I grew wings,

Wings

of freedom, to fly at will, and sometime,

Time

Brings me back, where my footsteps I hear,

Here.

36. Dusk

A serene stillness slowly spreads its wings

As dusk descends to disperse day's turmoils,

The birds in flocks crowd with fluttering wings,

A serene stillness slowly spreads its wings.

The trees stand as though waiting in the wings

Alive with the chatter of daily toils,

A serene stillness slowly spreads its wings,

As dusk descends to disperse day's turmoils.

37. The Gulmohur Tree

Can I still hope to see you tomorrow?

Beneath the great flaming Gulmohur tree,

Near the crystal pond where the lilies grow,

Can I still hope to see you tomorrow?

As I stand here now I miss you so,

The golden moon's up and it's you I see.

Can I still hope to see you tomorrow,

Beneath the great flaming Gulmohur tree?

38. Ode to Night

When you step in through the clouds of evening colours,

When the sounds and sights of day come under your spell,

I watch you as in a trance,

The ethereal beauty that is yours till the first flush of dawn.

Silent Night, don't pass me by even though

I hear your fleeting footsteps outside my window

Let me listen to your silence---

To your lullaby, in the cool quiet air ---

Let me watch the fireflies in their luminous forms

As you dance with the shadows in the bubbling brook.

Let me sing your praise when the half moon bathes you in silver light

And joins you in your moment of leisure on mountains high,

And, beneath your watchful eye let me dream.

Dark Night, as you tiptoe by in your velvet veil, lighting up the stars, pause awhile,

Let me feel your mystery in the misty air,

The sense of peace and quietude,

The promise of yet another morn.

Let me float like a feather tossed from heaven

And behold your world of silhouettes from above,

In the streaming rain or, in the flash of lightning,

And then from your velvet lap let me feel

The tingling touch of the ocean wave as it rises to
the rhythm

Of a million thunderous beats and falls in foaming
rapture

To cast me like a stray shell on the cool sandy
beach.

Sweet Night, slow down your pace,

Sit by my side, just you and I,

And fill me with your fragrance,

Show me what I see not in the glaring light of day

Let me lay at your feet all my thoughts and troubles

Of mundane struggles---.

Stop! Hold your breath,

Listen to me, while I my prayers say

And in my prayers help me see

A glimpse of blissful eternity.

39. Seasons and Fruits

Each season brings fruits of great variety,

Each fruit, each tree, strings of endless memories,

Of seasons spent with cool spiced drinks, fragrant
tea,

Of monsoon moods and those springtime agonies.

The pears, apples, oranges, the strawberry,

The humble guava, banana, the litchis

More, but, close to my heart as summer draws
near,

It's the mango, the mango I hold most dear.

But now that winter is stopping by again

I live in hope of fruition of my wishes,

Before the fleeting winter is on the wane

Be blessed by the date palm tree's honeyed graces,

Made from the early morning sap, its fine strain

Delights the heart, sweetens time one cherishes.

So much fruition from Nature's abundant store

Let's hail each season with gratitude and more.

40. Life and Death

Life:

As long as I am, Death shall keep constant vigil,

While I in my gay, careless mood shall flit about

Like a floating lamp passing through shadow and doubt.

My effervescence self shall dance to my free will,

Sing songs that will fill earth and every distant hill

And move great oceans and mountains to touch the cloud,

And smile up at the sky above and shout out loud,

I am infinite breath that death can never still!

I wonder about that lingering presence

In the shadows, sly, or bold as sunlight's kiss,

My joyous hours and melancholic moments

Grow dim as threatening clouds shadow my bliss.

Ah, Death! Grand in disguise, on a black charger,

Shall come, his grandeur dimmed by Life's surrender.

Death:

On stealthy steps in silence, silence I wear.

I move unseen through Life's meandering ways.

I'm here, right here, as long as nights turn to days.

Robust Life, prance on with every breath you bear,

You are, so I'm. You reap name, the same I share,

You light up the cosmos, yours a dream of haze,

I'm stark! Bold? Counting seconds the sun's rays?

Arise Truth. Claim me as your own if you dare.

That span of time between you and another,

That is where I abide as a guiding light.

Every throb I mark till the appointed hour

And then I blind you with my unwelcome sight.

Dear Life, your cup's full; let it flow without care,

Curse me, but I'm answer too, to a prayer.

41. A War is on.

Close your eyes and shut your ears

The world's gone mad, quell your fears

Shout out your anger

Shed no tears

The world's gone mad,

Quell your fears.

No more music in the wind

No more voice calling from behind.

No sound of laughter

No one smiled

All stunned with anger

No one cried.

Close your eyes and shut your ears

The world's gone mad, stop your tears

Birds crouch, missiles fly

Great guns roar

Power is sly,

Hurrah War!

The earth's bounty knows no bounds

Enough for all, enough for hounds

What's right, what's wrong

Messed up sore

Like a mashed up song

Oh, War.

Close your eyes and shut your ears

The world's gone mad, hold your fears

Shut out your anger

Stop the tears

Stop the bloodshed

Stop the fears.

Politics keeps ticking on

Power and might are close and strong

Greed stands alongside

Humming her sly old song.

Close your eyes and shut your ears

The worlds gone mad,

A war is on.

42. Bumble Bee

Bumble Bee went to tea

On a hot summer's day

When the clock struck at three

She tiptoed all the way.

The wind was a blowing

The trees were upside down

The lizard held a ring

To the fly in silken gown.

Bumble Bee, Bumble Bee,

They said in a chorus,

Sip your tea, watch and see

Your bridegroom in a bus.

Bumble Bee danced in glee

And buzzed and fussed for long

Took a dip in the sweet, sweet tea,

And broke out in a song.

The tea was in the cup

The cup stood on the wall

The Bee gave a hiccup

The tea flew down the wall.

43. Pink Missiles

Oh come, come come,

Let's go for a ride

On pretty little missiles

That waltz through the night.

Like fairies that glide

With wings so bright

Oh, come, come, come

Let's go for a ride.

Let's sit on the air

And jump up and down

And feed on bomb chops

With mayonnaise in our hair.

Let's dance in the smoke

Munch bullets on the stair

Let's tip toe on trees

And chase a crimson hare.

Oh, come, come, come

Let's go for a ride

On pretty pink missiles

That zoom through the night.

44. Who?

The still, brooding water

Like sudden sparks, scatter

As if someone has just thrown

In playful mood a little stone.

I sit on the damp, flattened grass and wonder,

Who else, before me has been here?

Who sits by this pool of darkness as I do now?

Who spreads the yellow leaves like a carpet?

Who?

Who breathes the putrid air that blows here?

Who else shares with me my melancholic hour

And treads on my pathway to this secret bower,

And hides when I appear?

Who?

I look around me in the gathering gloom,

I breathe the silence surrounding me,

Its ripples now fading into eternity

Leaving me to wonder — who else is here with me.

45. Betrayal

Betrayal! May this ugly human flaw burn!

Lowest of the low used to inflict for lust,

For greed of land, for immoral possession,

Destroyer of friend and friendship, burn it must.

Lowest of the low used to inflict for lust

Wrongfully aimed to maim a rich dwelling place

Destroyer of friend and friendship, burn it must,

Reduced to ashes without any trace.

Wrongfully aimed to maim a rich dwelling place

Wrecking a dear friend's home to smithereens

Reduced to ashes without any trace,

Shattering in seconds all fond memories.

Wrecking a dear friend's home to smithereens

Waging wars with the docile with deadly ease

Shattering in seconds all fond memories

Forgetting all lessons learnt on mother's knees.

Waging wars with the docile with deadly ease

For greed of land, for immoral possession,

Forgetting all lessons learnt on mother's knees,

Betrayal! May this ugly human flaw burn!

46. Death in a Submarine

I'm one of many, keeping vigil
A million metres under the sea
I work by the clock with my team
My home my nation's submarine.

I long for the sun, the air and the sky
And the green, green earth below my feet
To hear the laughter of my child
To feel the love of my family.

We have been trained to tame the sea,
Survive in the face of calamity,
As man, man's machine we're proud to man
Against man's machine in the deep, deep sea.

But can the sea be tamed? No never.
It has a mighty force of its own
Dark and ominous, I quell my fear
My training allows me no more.

And now I know death hovers near

I can read it on faces around me

The sea has entered the nation's pride

In spite of the SOS from the sea.

We count our seconds in helpless anger

As our President talks and nods

And decides if help is what we need

Or awards for heroism at sea.

I write at random, I write in the dark,

I gasp for breath and think of home

I smile to myself if this is Death

Then what is Life if the sea is my home?

I rise above the icy depths

My loved ones I wish so much to see

They pray with anguish in their hearts

For the encapsulated young lives

Doing duty in the deep, deep sea.

47. An Epistle

Dear Mr. Know All,

I know you know all that there's to know,

But what you do not know is the way

To your house, which we frequent

Through the seasons,

Through moonlight and dark.

It starts right from the clock tower

In the old bazaar,

Goes past old Lisamma's house

By the lotus lake,

And winds up the rocky hill through

The nodding lantana bushes,

Turns sharply right, then slopes down

Towards a rivulet, that shines bright

Like a strip of Mercury.

Another turn,

And behold, there's your house.

Tall and pretty commanding the view,

Studded with traffic lights and what not.

We wait in silence as you lock up

And drive away in your swanky car

For some fun filled hour,

While we slip in through your kitchen window

And enjoy the luxury of your spa.

Your lush house is ours

For a few magic hours.

Do you know that, Mr. Know All?

But thank you, thank you so much.

48. Winter

Come Winter, season of goodwill and festive spirit,

Come to us, throw your misty veil over hills and vales

Come and sit on the window top, on the garden green,

Come let us talk together as the sun sinks unseen.

Winter, you've been late this year, your footsteps have been slow

Your cloak of white has lost its sheen, the trees stand demure

Much chaos on this earth has broken your solitude

So you stand in the sidelines, unsure of what to do.

This war-torn earth bleeds so, your snow cannot hide the wounds

Your cool, crisp breath cannot quell the hate and fear that rules

Nor stop the fire, fumes of guns, nor calm the wails of war.

Yes Winter, let Autumn pass, it's your turn like before.

Let pretty flowers bloom again, that wilt in summer sun

Let winter crops grow and thrive, let rivers flow and run.

Let festive joys light up the lives of one and everyone

Come Winter, spend your time with us, till your turn is done.

49. The Wizened old Man

In a melancholic state of mind one day

When I had just bid farewell to a loved one,

The puzzle of life and after-life did crowd my mind

As I looked for answers I couldn't find.

Wandering there in the crowded street

That lined the river where souls did meet

I chanced upon a wizened old man

Whose hawk like eyes beckoned me.

Thus drawn to him, I sat on his stool

And gazed at him in speechless awe,

What brings you here, he said to me,

What is it you want to know?

When --- when is my end? I stammered,

That's all--- that's all I need to know for now ---.

I held his gaze, as he held mine

Through rimless glasses, his eyes they shone

Like lightning they bore into my soul

As he coughed the words in mocking tone,

That's all, huh, that's all you need to know?

Seconds passed, I sat still,

Trembling like a leaf in an autumn wind,

There's no end, no end, no end,

His voice like whiplash struck me,

A bony finger shaking at me---

Life spins the wheel of fortune and doom till eternity

Countless ends end in life itself

When egos play and have their way.

Countless beginnings regain life

When truth is allowed to show the way.

Every moment is an end and a beginning

It is you alone who can make your way,

An end can be a bend you know,

Before you see, or miss the light ahead.

Away, away, go find your way, make your end along the way.

50. My Muse and me

Restless in every limb, aimless in vacant state,

Hair disheveled, brows furrowed deep, you wait

For that perfect word, that hue, that elusive gait.

How beautiful is solitude covered in misty light

How beautiful is the silence that rules the starry night

How beautiful is the mind that can sort all thoughts tonight.

Come, sit by my shore and you will know solitude,

Leave all your thoughts behind and I will change your mood.

Watch me flow, flow, and together let us brood.

Ah, Solitude, I seek you in every nook and corner,

In ancient palaces, in every secret bower,

In the softest light of dawn, in evening's quiet hour.

In the softest light of dawn, noon or twilight, ---
don't fret so

Sort out your thoughts and lay them out in a neat
row.

Look up. The hues are there, choose the words you
know.

The world is a muddle; all feelings have gone for
a toss,

Simple things so jumbled up, for words I am at a
loss.

Oh, an hour of solitude to free my tangled thoughts.

Now dear poet, holder of pen, brush, chisel,

Sit by my muddy shore and try to be still

Surrender to beauty and let your heart fill.

You flow in quiet contentment, your ripples a soft
sigh,

You play so rough when clouds come up, you swell
up so high,

And heave and roll in mirth, as the moon glides up
the sky.

There you are, now find your way as I do mine own

Down deep valleys green, to nestle in rocks birds have known

Do not whine, do not pine, be free to create alone.

I shall I shall, I hear you. My Muse at last speaks to me

No more, no more, in vacant state will you ever find me

Come, come my noble pen, let's feel together what we see.

The End.